A souvenir guide

Rudyard Kipling at Bateman's

East Sussex

National Trust

'A Good and a Peaceable Place'

'We have loved it ever since our first sight of it ... We entered and felt her Spirit – her Feng Shui – to be good. We went through every room and found no shadows of ancient regrets, stifled miseries, nor any menace, though her new end was three hundred years old ... A real house in which to settle down.'

Kipling, 1902

Fame and misfortune

When he brought his family here in September 1902, Rudyard Kipling was already world famous. *The Jungle Book* had been translated into many languages, and the more recent *Kim* was recognised as a masterpiece. However, the death of his beloved elder daughter Josephine in 1899, at the age of only six, had combined with the pressures of public interest in his private life to drive him away from his first Sussex home, in Rottingdean. Bateman's offered him the chance to live quietly as an English country landowner.

Rudyard and his wife Caroline had first seen the house in 1900 and they were both immediately attracted to it, but it was let to someone else before they could make an offer. So when the house came back on the market in the summer of 1902, they were determined to have it. Kipling paid £9,300 for the house, various outbuildings including a mill, and 33 acres (13.3 hectares) of land.

An English idyll

For Kipling, Bateman's represented his ideal of England. It had been built in 1634, of local, traditional materials: Ardingley sandstone had been quarried nearby to make the walls; local clay was dug and fired to supply the brickwork and the roof tiles; oak had been cut from the woods to make beams and floor boards; and the metal hinges and window catches were forged from Wealden iron. All had mellowed delightfully with the passage of time, but had otherwise changed very little. Indeed, the house lacked even the most basic of modern conveniences: there was no running water upstairs or electricity. Nevertheless, the setting was perfect – hidden

Left Rudyard Kipling in 1891; painted by John Collier

away in the gently sloping, wooded landscape of the Dudwell valley, where he would not be bothered by persistent admirers. Also, significantly, Kipling did not have to scratch very far below the surface of the Sussex Weald to reveal rich seams of English history.

'Behold us the lawful owners of a grey stone lichened house – AD 1634 over the door – beamed, panelled, with old oak staircase, and all untouched and unfaked…. It is a good and a peaceable place standing in terraced lawns nigh to a walled garden of old red brick and two fat-headed old oast-houses with red brick stomachs, and an aged silver grey oak dovecot on top.'

Kipling, letter to Charles Eliot Norton, December 1902

Left The south door

Above The Kiplings at the south door of Bateman's

Some Key Dates

Left Kipling in 1898; etching by William Strang, who was fascinated by the macabre side of Kipling's work. Strang illustrated Kipling's *Thirty Short Stories* (1905)

1865	Rudyard Kipling born on 30 December in Bombay
1871–7	Fostered in Southsea: 'The Years of Desolation'
1878–82	At school at United Services College, Westward Ho!
1882–9	On staff of *Civil and Military Gazette*, Lahore, and then to the *Pioneer*, Allahabad
1888	*Plain Tales from the Hills*
1889–92	Literary acclaim in London
1892	Marries Caroline Balestier on 18 January in London Josephine Kipling born on 29 December, in Vermont, USA
1894	*The Jungle Book*
1896	Elsie Kipling born on 2 February, in Vermont
1897	Returns to England and settles in Rottingdean John Kipling born on 17 August
1899	Josephine dies of pneumonia on 6 March in New York *Stalky & Co.*
1901	*Kim*
1902	**Moves to Bateman's** *Just So Stories*
1906	*Puck of Pook's Hill*
1907	Nobel Prize for Literature
1910	*Rewards and Fairies*
1915	John missing, presumed killed, at the Battle of Loos
1923	*The Irish Guards in the Great War*
1924	Elsie marries George Bambridge
1936	Dies on 18 January in London
1937	*Something of Myself*
1939	Caroline Kipling dies, bequeathing Bateman's to the National Trust as a memorial to her late husband
1976	Wimpole Hall bequeathed to the National Trust by Elsie Bambridge

The Most Famous Writer in the British Empire

'If you can talk with crowds and keep your virtue,
Or walk with Kings – nor lose the common touch...
Yours is the Earth and everything that's in it,
And – which is more – you'll be a Man, my son!'

Kipling, 'If–', from *Rewards and Fairies*

Kipling was born in Bombay in 1865, the son of John Lockwood Kipling (who taught in that city's school of art) and of Alice Macdonald, whose sisters married the painters Edward Burne-Jones and E.J. Poynter and the ironmaster and politician Alfred Baldwin. Kipling was fostered back in England, where he was initially miserable. Having been removed from the foster home, he was happier at the United Services College, Westward Ho!, in Devon (the inspiration for *Stalky & Co.*). On returning to India, he rapidly made a reputation as a journalist, writing satirical verses and stories about the lives of the English of all classes, who sustained the British Raj. Collected verse in *Departmental Ditties* (1886), and stories in *The Railway Library*, followed by *Plain Tales from the Hills* (1888), established him as a powerful new literary voice.

Kipling returned to England in 1888, determined to make a career as a writer. Fluent and immensely hardworking, he was an instant success, and soon had little reason to worry about money. (His lifetime literary earnings, from hardback books alone, have been estimated to be about £1 million.)

In 1892 he married Caroline Balestier, the sister of an American publisher friend. They settled on the Balestier estate in Vermont, where their two girls, Josephine, and Elsie, were born. However, Kipling fell out with his brother-in-law and, pilloried for this by the American press, returned to England, where their son John was born in 1897. In 1899 they were shattered by Josephine's sudden death from pneumonia, while on a visit to New York. Finding English winters unsupportable, from 1900 to 1908 they spent winter holidays in South Africa, at the invitation of Cecil Rhodes, who influenced Kipling's imperialist world view.

Opposite **Kipling at work in 1885/6**

Right **Kipling in 1894; cartoon by Sir Leslie Ward ('Spy')**

Above *Soldiers Three*; plaque designed by Kipling's father, John Lockwood Kipling

Kipling's reputation

Kipling was immensely popular with a wide public, but he never appealed much to liberal literary critics, who were uncomfortable with his defiant defence of the British Empire, his use of 'vulgar' speech patterns, and his interest in the work of the common man. He was both prolific and various, achieving success in almost every literary genre, from novels and short stories to poetry, essays and satires. Some of his creations, such as the combination of prose and verse in collections like *Puck of Pook's Hill,* almost defy categorisation. T. S. Eliot found this form fascinating. His poem 'If–' still stirs the heart and lodges in the memory, but it is his writing for children that has perhaps lasted best, because it is so vivid and immediate. Most people now know Kipling from the Disney cartoon realisation of *The Jungle Book,* which has little to do with the original. How he would have responded to it, we cannot say, but we should remember that he was one of the first great writers to contemplate and collaborate on film versions of his work.

Today, Kipling may seem like an establishment figure, but he never sought official recognition of his work. He accepted the Nobel Prize for Literature in 1907 (the first British writer, and still the youngest, to receive it), but refused a knighthood and the Order of Merit, because of his suspicion of politicians. 'I prefer to live and die just Rudyard Kipling'.

'In the High and far-off Times, the Elephant, O Best Beloved, had no trunk …'

Kipling, 'The Elephant's Child', from *The Just So Stories*

Settling down: 'The Very-Own House'

'Men and women may sometimes, after great effort, achieve a creditable lie; but the house, which is their temple, cannot say anything save the truth of those who have lived in it.'

Kipling, *Traffics and Discoveries* (1904)

For Kipling, Bateman's represented all that was best about traditional England, and he furnished it with a mixture of old oak pieces and Arts and Crafts objects conceived in the same spirit. Comfort was not a high priority, but he did not enjoy dreary English winters, and so, in a concession to modern convenience, he asked his architect cousin Ambrose Poynter to install electricity. This was generated by a turbine in the water mill, and produced enough power to light ten 60-watt bulbs. Poynter also provided bathrooms and modern plumbing. (The house had none when the Kiplings moved in.)

After four decades of a nomadic life, Kipling was keen to settle down at Bateman's. Here he could write in privacy, enjoy his children and have his friends and relations to stay. In the 1920s there were, on average, about 150 visitors a year. He gradually acquired more and more of the surrounding woods and fields in the Dudwell valley to keep the curious at bay,

Below The Bateman's visitors' book. The initials 'FIP' indicate those unhappy guests that 'Fell in pond'.

Below left Kipling's very own Eden: the Dudwell valley

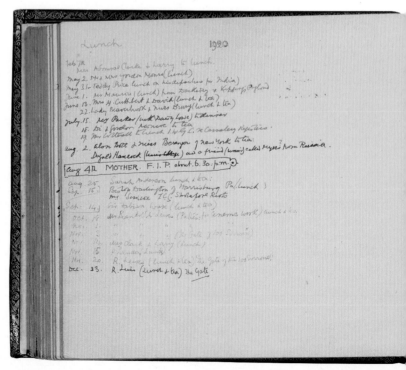

and to enjoy his interests as a gentleman farmer. He kept herds of Guernsey dairy cows and Sussex beef cattle, partly as ornaments for the landscape. He was also very keen on pigs, but again, perhaps, because it was the proper thing to do rather than to make money. At Christmas 1919, he gave his cousin Stanley Baldwin a little wooden pig, complete with a poem that begins:

Some to Women, some to Wine –
Some to Wealth or Power incline,
Proper people cherish Swine.

'England is a wonderful land. It is the most marvellous of all foreign countries that I have ever been in. It is made up of trees and green fields and mud and the Gentry: and at last I'm one of the Gentry!'

Kipling, November 1902

'For rest and refreshment and dearly-loved experiments and anxieties, during the six months or so of each year that we stayed in England, there was always the House and the land, and on occasion the Brook at the foot of our garden, which would flood devastatingly.'

Kipling, Something of Myself (1937)

Above Kipling's desk in the Study

Inspired by Bateman's

'Of all the trees that grow so fair,
Old England to adorn,
Greater are none beneath the Sun,
Than Oak, and Ash, and Thorn.'

Kipling, *Puck of Pook's Hill* (1906)

Kipling was seldom happier than when hidden away at Bateman's, but he was also a pioneer motorist who enjoyed exploring England by car. As he remarked, 'The chief end of my car is the discovery of England... To me it is a land full of stupefying marvels and mysteries.' Several of Kipling's later works were inspired by the landscape and history of this part of Sussex. In the summer of 1904 the family prepared a performance of Shakespeare's

Above Kipling in 1900; painted by John Collier

Left Kipling's 1928 Rolls-Royce Phantom. It cost him £2,833 18s. 6d

A Midsummer Night's Dream in the Quarry Garden, and the closeness of 'Pook's Hill' to his property combined with the Shakespearean spirit, 'Puck', to spark an idea. John played the part of Puck, Elsie was Titania, and Kipling played Bottom. Puck serves as a magical link for the 21 historical tales that make up *Puck of Pook's Hill* and *Rewards and Fairies*, ranging in date from the Roman invasion to the French Revolution. John and Elsie appear in the stories, as Dan and Una, but the hero is Hobden, the local hedger, who for Kipling symbolised the continuity of past and present Sussex.

Rewards and Fairies, published in 1910, was also written for Kipling's children, but some of the stories have a distinctly more adult tone. Kipling was very conscious of the difficulties of writing for two audiences:

Since the tales had to be read by children, before people realised that they were meant for grown-ups … I worked the material in three or four overlaid tints and textures, which might or might not reveal themselves according to the shining light of sex, youth and experience.

Kipling was close to his children and would read aloud to them and their friends for hours in a clear, expressive voice.

Left Puck helping Wayland, Smith of the Gods, to forge a sword; engraving from the 1909 edition of *Puck of Pook's Hill*

Life at Bateman's

The day began at 6.30, when the kitchenmaid would light the fire in the kitchen to make tea for the staff. At 7.30 the head housemaid would take tea up to the Kiplings' bedroom and to any guests who were staying. The housemaids would then carry up pails of hot water for washing. Kipling washed and shaved in his own bathroom, or used the 'powder room' over the porch. Mrs Kipling used a washstand in the cubicle off their bedroom. In winter, as he grew older, Kipling was a late riser, staying in bed until 10.00 if he was feeling poorly. While the family was having breakfast, which was served at 8.30, the under-housemaid cleaned and tidied the bedrooms and bathrooms. Only the head housemaid was allowed to tidy the Study. At 10.00, Mrs Kipling would discuss the day's menus with the cook, who had already checked with the head gardener what fresh fruit and vegetables were available from the garden. Dry groceries and wine were issued from a locked cupboard outside the kitchen.

The housemaids' morning uniform comprised a blue or pale grey cotton dress, with a white apron and cap, and black stockings and shoes. After lunch, which was served at 1.00, they changed into a black alpaca dress with white collar and cuffs, and smaller cap and apron.

Right Caroline (Carrie) Kipling, who ran the household with great efficiency

by two housemaids and a kitchenmaid. A lady's maid looked after all Mrs Kipling's needs, while the parlourmaid served food in the Dining Room. All the servants 'lived in' at the west end of the house, eating together in the servants' hall and sleeping in bedrooms above. They also had the use of a bathroom, which was installed when the Kiplings moved in. In the 1920s the under-housemaid was paid £26 per year with meals and board included. The outside staff comprised the chauffeur, who drove Kipling's beloved Rolls-Royce, the head gardener and 4–5 other gardeners, and an odd-job man.

Afternoon tea was served in the Parlour, or in front of the fire in the Hall. While dinner was being served, usually at 8.00, the under-housemaid would prepare the bedrooms for the night, turning down the sheets and drawing the curtains. Throughout their time at Bateman's, the Kiplings would dress formally for dinner.

The staff

Kipling employed a secretary to handle his huge correspondence, and to type up his writings. There was also a governess, when the children were young (John went off to boarding school when he was 10). Mrs Kipling ran the household with great efficiency, so there was no need for a butler or a housekeeper. The senior member of staff was the cook, Mrs Richardson, who was supported

'And whoever wakes in England
Hears, each morning, on the stair
The bathroom pipes in earnest spate,
And the she-cook calling the
    plumber's mate
In England now!'

Kipling (after Robert Browning), in a letter
to Sir Henry Newbolt, April 1929

Left Ewer, basin and chamberpot in John's Bedroom

Below The oast house was converted into staff quarters

'My Boy Jack'

Above John Kipling in his Irish Guards uniform

'"Have you news of my boy Jack?"
Not this tide.
"When d'you think that he'll come back?"
Not with this wind blowing, and this tide.'

Kipling, *My Boy Jack* (1916)

Kipling had grimly predicted the outbreak of the First World War and, as soon as hostilities were declared, he put himself at the service of the State. His publishers, Macmillan, produced a pocket-size Service Edition of his work for the comfort of the troops. His son John's first attempt to join the army was rejected because of poor eyesight, though John was determined that he would serve his country. Under some pressure, Kipling pulled strings with a friend in the army high command, General Lord Roberts, and secured his son a commission in the 2nd Battalion of the Irish Guards.

A year later, at 5.30 on the afternoon of 25 September 1915, John wrote from the front:

'Just a hurried line as we start off tonight … This will be my last letter most likely for some time as we won't get any time for writing this next week, but I will try & send Field post cards.

Well so long old dears.
Dear love
John.'

It was his last letter. After two days of bitter fighting at Loos, initial Allied advances were faltering, and the Guards Division was committed among the final reserve, but to no avail. On 2 October, the Kiplings received a telegram from the War Office, announcing that their son was listed as missing in action. The news was a crippling blow, but Kipling refused to give way to his grief, clinging on for a while to the increasingly forlorn hope that

John had been taken prisoner. Eventually, John had to be counted among the 20,000 British soldiers who had died in this engagement. In his 1916 poem *My Boy Jack* (ostensibly written about Ship's Boy Jack Cornwell VC, and other 'Jack Tars') Kipling records his own loss. He couldn't face attending the dedication of the war memorial in Burwash which bears John's name, though he later paid for a bugler to sound the Last Post at dusk each evening at the Menin Gate. This is the memorial to the Allied dead who have no known grave. He could take no pleasure in victory, when it was finally declared in 1918.

'That flesh we had nursed from the
   first in all cleanness was given
To corruption unveiled and assailed
   by the malice of Heaven –
By the heart-shaking jests of Decay
   where it lolled in the wires –
To be blanched or gay-painted by
   fumes – to be cindered by fires –
To be senselessly tossed and
   retossed in stale mutilation
From crater to crater. For that we
   shall take expiation.
But who shall return us our children?'

Kipling, *The Children*

Above John Kipling (third from left in glasses) during officer training in 1915

Left Kipling in the trenches in 1915

Last years

Among the surviving guardsmen Kipling befriended, in the course of writing the book, was Captain George Bambridge, who married his younger daughter Elsie. Elsie was devoted to her father, despite being conscious that she could never replace her departed siblings. It was she who, with her mother's help, supervised publication of the great Sussex edition of his works and, following her mother's wishes, gave Bateman's to the National Trust in 1939, as a permanent memorial to her father.

The Kiplings continued to entertain their small circle of friends at Bateman's in the post-war years, but the atmosphere was inevitably melancholy. The loss of their only son was a source of unassuageable grief. Kipling tried to ease his pain by throwing himself into the work of the Imperial War Graves Commission. He served as the Commission's literary adviser, choosing the form of words that was to be used in the British war cemeteries: 'Their name liveth for evermore' (from Ecclesiasticus 44:14) on the Stone of Remembrance; and 'A Soldier of the Great War Known unto God' on the gravestones of those whose bodies could not be identified. Kipling also accepted the invitation to write the Great War history of his son's regiment. When he came to describe John's death, it is buried in a list of the seven other Irish Guards officers who were killed or injured the same day. He concluded with impossible stoicism: 'It was a fair average for the day of a debut, and taught them somewhat for their future guidance.'

Right Kipling with George V

Left Elsie Kipling with her husband, Captain George Bambridge, at Wimpole Hall

The young novelist Rupert Croft-Cooke visits Kipling at Bateman's in 1922:
'At 57, with his vast bushy eyebrows greying, his thick glasses and his bald pate, he attracted all my adolescent reverence towards a father figure, yet the little legs in plus-fours, the shortness, and something impish which instantly appeared, wiped out my awe and shyness.'

The Kiplings' emotional torment was matched by their continuing physical ailments. Kipling was suffering from an undiagnosed duodenal ulcer and Carrie from diabetes. Kipling was less productive than he had been in his earlier years, but he wrote speeches and Christmas broadcasts for King George V, who died two days after he did. The pallbearers at Kipling's funeral included the Prime Minister, Stanley Baldwin (Rudyard's cousin). His ashes were interred in Poets' Corner in Westminster Abbey beneath a tablet that was inscribed simply: 'RUDYARD KIPLING'.

Exploring Bateman's

'Alive with ghosts and shadows.' Kipling

'You walk up to the porch over a stone-paved path laid down in the turf and the cartroad runs within fifty yards of the front door. The rest is all fields and farms and to the southward one glorious sweep of woods.'

The house was built in 1634 (the date over the Porch) for William Langham, a London merchant who lived here until his death in 1652. It is constructed from finely cut blocks of locally quarried sandstone, which are streaked with iron. The window frames and mullions are also carved in stone, in which are lead-glazed windows. The roof-scape is enlivened with tall red-brick chimneystacks. In very wet weather, the Dudwell has flooded as far as the house.

The Porch

On the left-hand side are carved the initials of the Kipling family: RK (Rudyard), CK (Carrie), EK (Elsie), JK (John). To the right of the front door hangs a wrought-iron bell pull that came from the home of Kipling's aunt, Georgiana Burne-Jones. It held many happy childhood memories for Kipling.

Above **The date Bateman's was built is carved above the Porch**

Left **The entrance gates**

The Hall
The Inner Hall

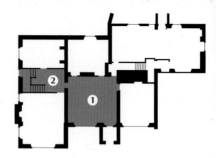

'There is a black and white tiled hall all panelled to the naked beamed cieling [sic] and the doors out of it have stone heads and old oak frames – dark as teak. There is a deep window seat and a high leaded window with lots of the old greeny-glass panes left and a flap-table of Queen Elizabeth's time … and benches and a stone arched fire place backed by old Sussex iron work. We burn wood in all the fires and the hall takes five foot logs.'

Kipling, November 1902

1 The Hall

The Hall immediately establishes the mood of the house – a mixture of the local and the exotic. The dark brown, well-worn panelling and the roughly carved stone doorways date back to the building of the house and were what first attracted the Kiplings to the house. The large Benares brass tray was a wedding present to the Kiplings from Rudyard's sister Trix. The Indian brass fish on wheels was a favourite toy, which John and Elsie played with almost to destruction.

Tea was often served on the Hall table. It usually consisted of thinly sliced bread and butter, spread with medlar jelly or blackcurrant jam, hot buttered scones and 'piles of home-made cakes'.

For more information on the furnishings and contents of Bateman's, go to: www.nationaltrustcollections.org.uk

Pictures

The watercolours include a view of the dining room at The Grange in 1904, when it was full of Morris & Co. furnishings of every kind. Kipling's uncle, E.J. Poynter, records the garden from the south-west, including the rectangular pond created by the Kiplings with the money he received for winning the Nobel Prize for Literature in 1907.

Left **The Hall**

Right **The view from the Inner Hall to the Hall**

The Hall features in Kipling's story 'They', which was written, with memories of his beloved daughter Josephine, soon after he settled at Bateman's:

> … a still, nut-brown hall, pleasant with late flowers and warmed with a delicious wood fire – a place of good influence and great peace…. A child's cart and a doll lay on the black-and-white floor, where a rug had been kicked back. I felt that the children had only just hurried away – to hide themselves, most like – in the many turns of the great adzed staircase that climbed stately out of the hall … An old eagle-topped convex mirror gathered the picture into its mysterious heart, distorting afresh the distorted shadows …

2 The Inner Hall

The staircase is made of oak (the 'Sussex weed', as it was known locally) and is mostly original, but the upper panels, which are lighter in colour, were added by Kipling.

Sculpture

Patrick Synge-Hutchinson's bronze bust of Kipling at the bottom of the stairs was not completed until after Kipling's death. The reliefs of Mowgli and the wolves (from *The Jungle Book*) and Kim were designed by Kipling's father. They were made from plaster painted to resemble bronze.

Right Patrick Synge-Hutchinson's bronze bust of Kipling

1 The Parlour

In the morning, Kipling's guests would use this room for reading or writing, while he worked upstairs in his Study. When the day's work was done, he would draw his chair up to the fire and sit and talk. In the evenings, it was the setting for uproarious parlour games – human and animal – which were described by Julia Taufflieb:

Here Rud would play with his dogs. Down on the floor in front of the fire Rud would throw himself, and the dogs always knew it was their hour. The rugs were turned up and a game of ball with Rud and the dogs was on the programme.

A phonogram plays music of the period, and Kipling's poetry set to music.

Above **The Parlour**

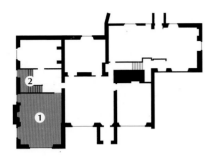

Furniture

Kipling furnished the house with traditional oak pieces or new Arts and Crafts replicas in the same style that made very little attempt at comfort. The green velvet-upholstered sofa was inspired by the famous 17th-century original at nearby Knole.

'The worst of the place is that it simply will not endure modern furniture.'

Kipling, 1902

2 The Staircase

The carved oak staircase and panelling mostly date from the building of the house in the 1630s. Centuries of polishing have turned them as 'dark as teak', as Kipling put it.

Tapestry

The 17th-century Brussels tapestry hanging on the stairs depicts the Queen of Sheba with her attendants.

Pictures

The portrait by John Collier on the half-landing shows Kipling in 1900, shortly before he bought Bateman's.

Above **The Staircase**

Left The 1912 Edison phonogram in the Parlour

The Study

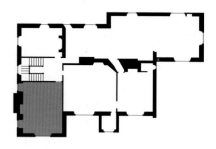

This was the heart of the house, where Kipling would retreat to write and read. He was an enviably fluent writer, but had to have all his writing tools and sacred relics arranged *just so*. The room has changed very little indeed since his day, but it has lost the pungent aroma of his Turkish tobacco (at times, he smoked 40 cigarettes a day).

'When writing verse, he usually paced up and down the study humming to himself.'

Elsie Bambridge

Desk: 'badly congested'
'I always kept certain gadgets on my work table, which was ten feet long from North to South and badly congested…..'

Oak day-bed
'Lying on his side, his head propped on his right hand, my father spent many hours on this sofa while he brooded over the work he was busy with at the moment. From time to time he would jump up and go to the desk, write a line or two, make a note or correction, then resume his place on the sofa.'

Elsie Bambridge

Below Kipling at his desk

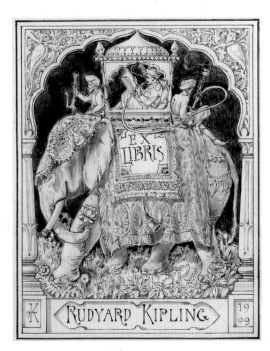

many inscribed presentation copies from admirers, such as Ernest Shackleton's *South*. Many of the books contain the handsome bookplate designed by his father, the watercolour study for which is on show in this room.

Pictures

The portrait over the fireplace of Carrie Kipling was painted by Kipling's cousin Philip Burne-Jones in 1899. She is shown with a key hanging from her waist. Carrie was a stern, but efficient mistress of the household, who paid all the bills and kept unwanted visitors at bay.

The master's voice

Although Kipling didn't die until 1936, there is only one known recording of him reciting his poetry; some audio and film clips are available in the NT archive.

Left Kipling's bookplate was designed by his father

Below The Study

Books

Kipling claimed that 'my treatment of books was popularly recorded as barbarian', but most of those preserved here are, in fact, in good condition. It is very much the working library of a professional writer, with few early or grand volumes.

G.O. Trevelyan's *The Competition Wallah* (1866) was awarded to him for winning a school poetry competition in which he was the only entrant. There is much else on India and the Far East.

As one would expect, the collection reflects Kipling's life at Bateman's and his other interests. So there are numerous books on the history of Sussex, on farming, bee-keeping and angling. His passion for tales of adventure encouraged him to acquire many books on the sea and the Royal Navy. His intense interest in the First World War, and its history, explains Friedrich von Bethardi's *How Germany makes War* (1914).

Although Kipling did not have many friends in the literary world, the Library includes

The West Bedroom
The Exhibition Room
John's Bedroom

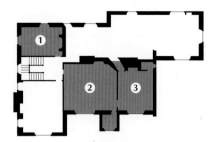

1 The West Bedroom

This guest bedroom has been presented as if being used by Kipling's cousin, the politician Stanley Baldwin, who was a frequent visitor to Bateman's.

2 The Exhibition Room

This room is used to display items from the rich Kipling archive, which was bequeathed to the National Trust by Elsie Bambridge, and which is on deposit at the University of Sussex. It may once have been the Kiplings' bedroom.

3 John's Bedroom

The Kiplings never recovered from the death of their son, but unlike some of those who had lost sons in the Great War, they did not turn his bedroom into a shrine. Most of John's possessions have long since been dispersed, but we have tried to suggest something of his personality in the furnishings of this room.

John was neither very academic nor very athletic, but was determined to do his best. Like most of his generation, when the First World War broke out in 1914, he enlisted without a moment's thought.

Right above **The West Bedroom**

Right **The Exhibition Room**

Pictures

The portraits of the Kiplings' children include a pastel of Josephine, who died in 1899 at the age of only six. Kipling's American publisher, Frank Doubleday, had the ghastly task of telling Kipling of her death: 'I told the story in as few words as I could. He listened in silence till I had finished, then turned his face to the wall.'

The three small caricatures are also of the Kipling children, and were drawn by their great-uncle Edward Burne-Jones at The Grange, over the Christmas of 1897.

Sculpture

The circular bronze relief of the Kiplings' youngest child Elsie was made by Henry Pegram in 1907. She was always conscious of the sorrow her parents endured from the loss of her siblings.

'The two great sorrows of their lives, my parents bore bravely and silently, perhaps too silently for their own good.'

Elsie Bambridge

Above Skis and football boots in John's Bedroom

Left Caricatures of Kipling's three children in 1897 by their great-uncle Edward Burne-Jones

The Dining Room
Elsie's Sitting Room

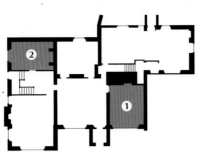

1 The Dining Room

The Kiplings took lunch at 1.00 and dinner at 8.00. Kipling had acquired a taste for spicy food during his time in India, but in later life he suffered from an agonisingly painful ulcer, which forced him to adopt a blander diet: steamed fish, chicken and junket were typical. The garden supplied a rich variety of fruit and vegetables. He offered his guests first-rate wines, but preferred to drink cider himself. Kipling was completely uninterested in clothes, preferring ancient tweeds for daily life, but he always dressed for dinner. At meal times the atmosphere was usually very informal: he loved feeding his two Aberdeen terriers with lumps of meat from the table despite the mess it made of his trousers and the carpet.

Wall-hangings

The 18th-century English leather wall-hangings in the Spanish 'Cordoba' style were bought in 1902 on the Isle of Wight, perhaps by Kipling's father. Leather wall-hangings of this kind were a traditional decoration for dining rooms, as they did not retain the smell of stale food in the same way as textiles.

Left The Dining Room

Right The heraldic cast-iron fireback in Elsie's Sitting Room. Firebacks like this were produced by the iron founders of the Sussex Weald

2 Elsie's Sitting Room

When the Kiplings first settled at Bateman's, they used this as a school room for their two children. Their first governess was a Miss Blaikie. In 1911 Dorothy Ponton was taken on to tutor John and Elsie. In 1912, when John was sent to a new boarding school, Wellington, this room was turned into a sitting room for Elsie, who lived at home until she married in 1924. As Elsie's parents grew older, she took on the responsibility of protecting them from unwanted visitors, much as Kipling had humorously acknowledged in a limerick written in 1911:
There was a young person of Bateman's
Who was guarded in most of her statements.
When they asked 'Where's your pa?'
She said – 'Out in his car'.
Whereas he was really in Bateman's.

A 1930s wireless broadcasts extracts from Kipling's life and poetry read by Ralph Fiennes.

Pictures

The five pictures on the wall above the panelling are watercolours by Kipling's father, depicting Indian people in various walks of life.

The Garden

Kipling 'designed it having in mind the house fitting into its surroundings like a lovely cup on a matching saucer.'
Elsie Bambridge on the garden

Bateman's appealed to Kipling as a natural haven of peace and seclusion away from the prying eyes of the public, sitting, as it does, in its own valley. He gradually bought the surrounding farm land, which now comprises the 300-acre (121 ha.) estate. Our tenant farmer looks after the field systems and our Ranger manages the hedgerows, footpaths and shaws (small areas of ancient woodland, sometimes featuring iron ore or clay pits, reminders of an earlier industrial heritage). The 12-acre (5 ha.) garden nestles comfortably in the centre of the estate.

The Orchard

This contains a nice mixture of apples, pears, plums, quince, medlar, crab apples and a black mulberry. All of these fruits and produce from the kitchen garden can be bought from the shop from mid-summer into autumn. The oldest fruit tree was the apple 'Beauty of Bath' (bottom corner by the end of the herb border), which was planted during Kipling's time, but which finally died in 2014. Before it failed, we took cuttings to graft on to a new root stock. Many of the existing trees may have been planted at the beginning of the Second World War, as much of the garden was turned over to the 'Dig for Victory' campaign at that time. Our veg plot is a remnant of this period.

The Orchard is divided by a hedge of heavenly smelling *Rosa rugosa* bearing giant hips in autumn. Along the west-facing wall is a cutting border, providing flowers and foliage for our floral displays in the house. We grow all our own vegetables and flowers from seed in the small greenhouse and cold frames, providing fresh vegetables and salad for the tea-room, and herbs from the Herb Border created by a former head gardener in the 1970s.

The Pear Allée

This was designed by Kipling to provide him with a long view down to the house. The ironwork and pear trees were taken down in 2007 as they had become intertwined. The framework was repaired and the original pear varieties replaced like-for-like. *Pulmonaria* (Lungwort) and *Brunnera macrophylla* (blue forget-me-not flowers) offer excellent ground cover in difficult places. *Epimedium alpinum* has small colourful leaves and flowers like tiny daffodils. In spring, the huge green leaves of *Colchicum autumnale* (Autumn crocus) appear. They absorb energy from sunlight which is stored in the bulb as food for the spectacular autumn show of chalice-like flowers, by which time the leaves will have disappeared. In summer geraniums provide colour below the developing pears, which leads us into autumn and the blooming of the crocus below the golden drooping pears.

Opposite **The vegetable garden**

Above **The Pear Allée**

The Mulberry Garden

Originally a cattle yard, the Mulberry Garden was laid out by Kipling in an arrangement of box-bordered beds, possibly in a kitchen garden style but certainly with a mixture of perennial and annual flowers as well. During the 1970s this garden was redesigned by Graham Stuart Thomas (NT garden adviser and author) as a mixed herbaceous and shrub area. We are now reviving a design closer to Kipling's original style of planting, creating a potager-style garden using structurally interesting plants as well as plants for cut flower and culinary use. The Black Mulberry tree (centre of lawn) is a replacement of Kipling's original tree.

There are several varieties of Clematis adorning the warm south- and west-facing walls including *C.* 'Perle d'Azur', *C.* 'Abundance' and the highly fragrant *C. montana* 'Grandiflora'. The paths here and elsewhere in the garden are interspersed with millstones; either solid millstone grits from Yorkshire or French burrs made from several pieces held together with iron bands. The metal gate in the Mulberry Garden was designed with stylised 'RK' lettering.

The Entrance Drive

The front hedge was a low field hedge when Kipling bought Bateman's. He replaced it and planted more hedges of yew to keep out prying eyes. The gates were originally wooden.

The Oast House

The Oast House, built in 1770, was converted into staff quarters by Kipling's cousin Ambrose Poynter. There was a servants' hall, and the cook lived upstairs.

Right **A view into the Mulberry Garden**

Above right
The Front Garden

The ground floor was originally a garage housing Kipling's Rolls-Royce and is now the shop, selling a range of new and secondhand Rudyard Kipling books, locally sourced produce, including honey from our own beehives, and plants from the garden.

Caught in the act

The story goes that one night one of the maids arrived back from the cinema in Heathfield to find the gate locked. She managed to heave her bike over the hedge and proceeded to climb over the gate. To her dismay Mr Kipling was walking the dog nearby and caught her in the act. He helped her over the gate, enquired why she was late and knowingly touched his nose with his finger. The next day, when he saw her, he winked to her, having kept the secret from his wife Carrie, who would not have been pleased if she had known about it.

The Front Garden

Kipling avoided any embellishment of the Front Garden. The ageing beauty of the house is echoed in the garden paths made of 'Sussex Marble': sedimentary muds laid down millions of years ago under tropical seas and containing fossilised shells. The ironstone slab by the front door is there 'to keep the witches out'. On the lawn to the right sits a Manna Ash (*Fraxinus ornus*), and to the left of the house is a bed of the delicious pink *Rosa* 'Maiden's Blush'.

Other plants of interest include several climbing roses: *Rosa* 'Goldfinch' and *Rosa* 'Ena Harkness', clematis and the climber *Actinidia kolomikta*, originally from the mountains of the Far East, with leaves that turn white and pink in the sun and small flowers smelling of Lily of the Valley. Also against the wall is an old pear tree thought to have been planted by Kipling.

Standing by the small iron gate in the Front Garden, you can glimpse the Donkey Field and Quarry Garden, which can be accessed via the Entrance Drive or by taking a pleasant stroll from Park Mill along the lane which borders the garden.

The Formal Garden (Quarterdeck)

The raised path and upper lawn that runs in front of the house is known as the Quarterdeck. Kipling was a frustrated naval man; his eyesight was too poor to enable him to become an officer, but during the winter the water levels around the River Dudwell rise, and the lower lawn is often flooded. So he may well have been able to stand on his quarterdeck and view the waters below.

More climbing plants adorn the walls of the house: *Wisteria sinensis* with its fragrant bright purple drooping racemes and, to the left, *Campsis grandiflora,* (the Trumpet Vine) bearing large orange/red tubular flowers in summer. Underneath this, the ornamental quince *Chaenomeles japonica* flowers in spring. In late spring the flowers of *Magnolia x soulangeana, M. x veitchii* and, in summer, *M. grandiflora* adorn the lawns around the main house and Oast House.

Turning towards the lower lawn terrace, we can see two perfectly straight rows of pleached limes, *Tilia platyphyllos* 'Rubra'. Planted in 1898, just before Kipling bought Bateman's, they are very much in keeping with the original Jacobean garden which must have existed here, this style of hedging being very fashionable during the 16th and 17th centuries. Surrounding this area of the garden are more tightly clipped yew hedges, all cut by eye and taking over two months to trim.

The Spring Borders

The two spring borders running along the western edge of the Quarterdeck are remnants of a larger series of beds that Kipling had planted around the edge of the Formal Garden. They provide the garden with a welcome splash of colour from February with red pulmonaria, hellebores and *Scilla siberica*. Primroses follow alongside the unusual green and black flower of the Widow Iris,

Hermodactylus tuberosus. Early summer-flowering shrubs such as *Salix hastata* 'Wehrhahnii', *Daphne x burkwoodii* and *Exochorda x macrantha* 'The Bride' take over, whilst interest continues with herbaceous perennials flowering between the shrubs in mid- to late summer.

The Lily Pond

In 1907 Kipling was awarded the Nobel Prize for literature, the first English-speaking author to win this accolade. With the prize he was awarded £7,770 (a sizeable sum in those days), which he used to create the Lily Pond and Rose Garden, just as you see them today.

FIP

The pond is a little over a foot and a half deep, shallow enough for Water Lilies to grow and for his children to swim in. He also had a flat-bottomed paddle boat built. If you look at the visitors' book in the house, you will see the cryptic initials FIP next to some people's names: Kipling's humorous way of noting the visitors who 'fell in the pond'. We now have a replica boat, which is brought out on sunny days for visitors to use on the pond and is managed through the hard work of our volunteers.

The Rose Garden

This was replanted in 2007, as the original plants were slowly dying. Two of the original floribunda varieties, 'Betty Prior' and 'Frensham', were replanted along with 'Valentine Heart' to replace 'Mrs Inge Poulsen', giving us a beautiful display of varying shades of pink throughout the summer. The two lead statues standing on stone plinths which Kipling had commissioned for the Rose Garden are figures of a boy and girl wearing Jacobean costumes, again harking back to the origins of the house and his own children.

The fish in the pond are Golden Orfe donated by Chartwell (the nearby home of Winston Churchill), and the small bubble fountain is gravity-fed from the Mill Pond beyond the Wild Garden. Before reaching the Wild Garden we can see the original stone laid in Westminster Abbey on Kipling's death.

Opposite **The Quarterdeck** in 1913; painted by E.J. Poynter

Above **The Rose Garden**

The Wild Garden

Leaving Kipling's original garden, as you pass between the stone pillars the atmosphere changes dramatically. This garden, where Kipling once had his tennis court, is now planted informally with a mass of spring bulbs and flowering trees and shrubs. We can highly recommend regular visits to admire the earliest snowdrops, narcissi, small blue *Scilla litardieri* and *S. bifolia* and the white gem-like flowers of Wood Anemones. Following swiftly on are the checkerboard-flowered Snake's Head Fritillary in purple and white, bluebells and the tall *Camassia leichtlinii* from North America carpeting the floor underneath the March-flowering *Cornus mas*, flowering cherries and the snowy peaks of *Amelanchier lamarckii* (Snowy Mespilus – Juneberry) in April and finally the Rhododendrons and sweet-smelling Azaleas and our remarkable flowering crab apple *Malus floribunda* in May to early June.

Standing on the first bridge over the River Dudwell, you can see the Skunk Cabbage (*Lysichiton americanum*), bearing giant acid yellow arum-type flowers (which give this plant the smelly part of its name) in spring. The river, although only 10 miles in length, is

Below The bridge in the Wild Garden

of very good quality and is host to a range of invertebrates, insects and fish, including nineteen Dragonfly, Damselfly and Demoiselle species, brown trout and Kingfishers, which can be seen darting over the water in summer. Just beyond the bridge is the tall Balsam Poplar, *Populus balsamifera*. In spring the sweet, musky perfume exuded from the opening leaf buds is quite intoxicating.

In summer, wild flowers take over from the cultivated species; Cuckoo Flower and Ramsons flower in abundance followed by a variety of vetches, clover and speedwells. Along the banks we can see Meadow Sweet

(*Filipendula ulmaria*) and Rosebay Willowherb, the living fossil that is Horsetail (*Equisetum*), which has been around for over 100 million years, and a mass of *Leucanthemum vulgare* (Ox Eye Daisies). By the bridge over the weir are the equally prehistoric-looking *Gunnera tinctoria,* Giant Rhubarb and *Darmera peltata* (Umbrella Plant). In late summer we take a hay cut in the Wild Garden and Meadow beyond, which helps to reduce the vigour of the grass, allowing more wild flowers eventually to colonise this area.

Above **The Wild Garden**

The Old Hay Meadow

This is a field taken back in-hand from our tenant farmers in 2010 and which we are restoring to a traditional wild flower hay meadow. This space is great for educating visitors, old and young, about nature, so we are creating a variety of habitats and providing fun, interactive activities such as pond-dipping and dragonfly- and butterfly-spotting. We have recently installed a new pond which is already being visited by dragonflies, frogs, newts and a range of invertebrates. There are also a surprising number of different wild flower species to be found here, including the nationally scarce Coralroot Bittercress.

Park Mill

The present mill was built about 1750 and extended in the 1830s. Kipling loved the idea of having a water mill in his garden, even if the first thing he did was to remove the wheel and have a turbine installed to generate electricity. Take a look around the Mill, and you can find out more about its origins, Kipling's plans for it, and the Trust restoration. The Mill still grinds wheat and you can buy our wholemeal flour, perfect for baking bread, here, in the shop or the ticket office.

The gate by the mill pond is the starting point for two of our estate walks, enabling you to experience the beautiful High Weald countryside and the hidden features of the landscape that inspired many of Kipling's later works, such as *Puck of Pook's Hill*.

The Quarry Garden

By following the footpath and lane to the left of the Mill Pond you will discover the Quarry Garden, recently excavated to expose the original rock face which we believe provided the sandstone blocks to build Bateman's. Clay for the tiles is abundant in the ground, and oak would have been taken from the Wealden estate for the beams and other woodwork. The surrounding area was a centre for the iron foundry industry in the 17th century, so metal fittings would have been local too. The Quarry Garden also contains Elsie's Memorial, a restoration of an earlier pavilion erected in memory of Kipling's younger daughter, who played a key part in helping the National Trust open Bateman's to the public. Kipling's children used to put on plays for friends and family in the Quarry Garden and you can imagine some of his greatest stories taking shape in such a setting.

The inspiration of *Puck of Pook's Hill*

'One summer in the early 1900s we children and my father acted scenes from *A Midsummer Night's Dream*. Our stage was an old grass-grown quarry, and there my brother as Puck, myself as Titania, and my father as Bottom, rehearsed and acted happily. A most realistic cardboard donkey's head had been donned by Bottom for his part, and the village policeman, passing along the lane, was amazed to see the familiar tweed-clad figure of my father topped by this extraordinary headgear.'

Elsie Bambridge

Follow the steps up to the left of the quarry and you will discover, in our opinion, the best view of the house and garden.

Opposite **Park Mill**

Above **Elsie's Memorial** in the Quarry Garden

The Donkey Field

Next door is the Donkey Field, so-called because the Kiplings kept a donkey here. The family were not greatly loved by the locals from Burwash, largely because Carrie had a fierce temper and never kept staff long. One night, so we are told, some of the locals crept into the field and painted the donkey white!

These days we manage this field by grazing with rare-breed sheep in autumn and winter and encourage wild flowers by taking an annual hay cut. In summer you can access the Donkey Field to enjoy such delightful plants as Yellow Rattle, Sheep's Sorrel, Common Knapweed and Bird's Foot Trefoil.

The Estate

The Bateman's estate consists of 300 acres (121 ha.) of beautiful High Weald countryside. Set within the High Weald Area of Outstanding Natural Beauty, this landscape is classically medieval; full of small fields, hedgerows, old trees, abandoned iron ore pits, hidden ponds and magical deserted trackways. The River Dudwell runs through the valley and there are seemingly endless magnificent views, making the Bateman's estate the perfect place for a restful, romantic stroll or an energetic hike with the family.

Kipling was inspired by this historic landscape to write some of his most famous works such as *Rewards and Fairies*. Read a poem such as *Alnaschar and the Oxen* and you'll realise it couldn't have been written anywhere else.

Longstanding tenant farmers graze a herd of beef cattle here, and some of the land is under Environmental Stewardship management. Explore the estate during spring and summer and you will see a host of butterflies, wild flowers such as green-winged orchids and bee orchids and bluebells, birdlife from wrens to buzzards, and damselflies and dragonflies flitting around ponds and river. During autumn and winter you will be treated to atmospheric mists, the golden hues of trees changing colour as they prepare to drop their leaves and the architectural elegance of the Weald's mighty oaks during winter.

The estate is the 'hidden gem' of Bateman's and as well as the network of footpaths that crosses it, there are now three waymarked walks to guide you around the area's beauty, history and landscape. These routes can be found in the Welcome Leaflet available at visitor reception.

Right **The wooded landscape to the west of the house**

Alnaschar and the Oxen

There's a pasture in a valley where the hanging woods divide,
    And a Herd lies down and ruminates in peace;
Where the pheasant rules the nooning, and the owl the twilight-tide
    And the war-cries of our world die out and cease.
Here I cast aside the burden that each weary week-day brings
    And, delivered from the shadows I pursue,
On peaceful, postless Sabbaths I consider Weighty Things –
    Such as Sussex Cattle feeding in the dew!

Kipling